INFORMATION
EXPLORER
JUNIOR

Find the Right Words with Thesauruses

by Kara Fribley

CHERRY LAKE PUBLISHING · ANN ARBOR, MICHIGAN

A NOTE TO PARENTS AND TEACHERS: Please remind your children how to stay safe online before they do the activities in this book.

CHERRY LAKE
Publishing

A NOTE TO KIDS: Always remember your safety comes first!

Published in the United States of America
by Cherry Lake Publishing
Ann Arbor, Michigan
www.cherrylakepublishing.com

Content Adviser: Gail Dickinson, PhD, Associate Professor, Old Dominion University

Book design and illustration: The Design Lab

Photo credits: Cover, ©iStockphoto.com/JenniferPhotographyImaging; page 5, ©iStockphoto.com/sefaoncul; page 7, ©iStockphoto.com/gbh007; page 15, ©tlorna/Shutterstock, Inc.; page 21, ©iStockphoto.com/Maica

Library of Congress Cataloging-in-Publication Data
Fribley, Kara.
  Find the right words with thesauruses/by Kara Fribley.
     p. cm.—(Information explorer junior)
  Includes bibliographical references and index.
  ISBN 978-1-61080-369-4 (lib. bdg.)—ISBN 978-1-61080-378-6 (e-book)—
ISBN 978-1-61080-394-6 (pbk.) 1. English language—Synonyms and
Antonyms—Juvenile literature. 2. Thesauri—Juvenile literature. I. Title.
  PE1591.F75 2012
  423'.12—dc23   2011034913

Cherry Lake Publishing would like to acknowledge
the work of The Partnership for 21st Century Skills.
Please visit www.21stcenturyskills.org for more information.

Printed in the United States of America
Corporate Graphics Inc.
January 2012
CLSP10

Table of Contents

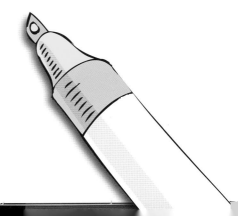

CHAPTER ONE

What Is a Thesaurus?

"Did you see those dinosaur bones? They were *big*!"

You chose the word "big" to describe the bones. But now you're not sure it was the right word. Another word might sound more exciting.

Look at those dinosaur bones! They are big!

The first word you think of is not always the best one to use.

4

How would you describe dinosaur bones to your friends?

Maybe you would rather say, "Those dinosaur bones were *gigantic*!" You said the exact same thing. But you just used "gigantic" instead of "big."

What are some other words that mean "big" or "gigantic"? You could try looking up "big" in the dictionary. A dictionary is a book or Web site that gives the **definitions** of words. A definition of a word is its meaning. But a definition won't always help you find a new word to use.

What you're really looking for is a **synonym** for the word "big." A synonym is a word that has the same meaning as another word. For example, "begin" is a synonym for "start." "Sad" is a synonym for "unhappy." Luckily, there is a tool that can give you all of the synonyms you need.

This tool is called a thesaurus. A thesaurus is also full of **antonyms**. These are words that have the opposite meaning of another word. "Small" and "tiny" are antonyms of "gigantic."

How will you remember the difference between synonyms and antonyms? Think of them this way:

Synonym = Same

Antonym = Opposite

A thesaurus also tells you the part of speech that a word is, such noun, verb, or adjective. The thesaurus gives you the definition of a word. It also includes

Using synonyms can help you avoid repeating the same word too many times.

Just exactly how do you say "thesaurus"? Just think of Tyrannosaurus rex. Replace the "tyranno" with the sound "thi." Now you've said it!

Say it like: thi-SAWR-uhs

thi + saurus

something called **related words**. These are words that are not *exactly* the same as the word you're looking up. But they are *almost* the same. Many times, a thesaurus will also give **near antonyms**. These are exactly what they sound like. They are *almost* the opposite of a word!

Activity

Let's sharpen your thesaurus skills! Tell whether each pair of words are synonyms or antonyms.

1. cold, freezing _____
2. top, bottom _____
3. sink, float _____
4. windy, calm _____
5. ill, sick _____
6. friend, enemy _____
7. speedy, fast _____

Write one complete sentence that uses two antonyms. Write another complete sentence that uses two synonyms. For both sentences, choose words that are different from ones listed above.

(Answers: 1. synonyms, 2. antonyms, 3. antonyms, 4. antonyms, 5. synonyms, 6. antonyms, 7. synonyms)

To get a copy of this activity, visit www.cherrylakepublishing.com/activities.

CHAPTER TWO

How to Use a Print Thesaurus

So, how do you use
this awesome tool
called a thesaurus?
A thesaurus can be either
a printed book or a Web site. First, let's learn
how to use a printed thesaurus.

    A thesaurus lists words alphabetically,
just like a dictionary. Let's say you want
to find a synonym or antonym for "walk."
Flip to the back of the book to the section
with the "W" words. Look at the top corner
of each page. The first and last word listed

on the page are given there. This makes it a little easier to find words in alphabetical order.

Every word will have information listed in a certain order. First, you will see the part of speech and the definition. Next is a list of synonyms. That is followed by a list of related words. The near antonyms come next. Finally, there is a list of antonyms. Here is what you might see for the word "walk":

word entry

Part of speech

definition

walk (verb) to move along by placing one foot on the ground before lifting the other

Synonyms: march, step, pace, stride

Related words: plod, stalk, patrol, parade

Near antonyms: trot, gallop, dart

Antonyms: run

These lists give you a lot of words to choose from. Did you see a word you especially like? You can use the thesaurus to look up that word!

What if a word you looked up doesn't have a list of synonyms or antonyms? Don't worry! The thesaurus can't list every synonym and every antonym for every word. Otherwise, the book would be too big to carry!

Instead, there is a note telling you to "see" another word. That word is a synonym for the one you looked up. It has a whole list of other synonyms for your word. It has a list of antonyms, too!

discover (verb) to find out
Synonyms: realize, learn, determine
see find

find (verb) to get something by chance or by searching for it
Synonyms: locate, come across, spot
see discover

To get a copy of this activity, visit www.cherrylakepublishing.com/activities.

Activity

BIG

1. Use a ruler to draw a line down the center of a page in your notebook. You should now have two long boxes.
2. Write "Synonyms for Big" at the top of the box on the left.
3. Write "Antonyms for Big" at the top of the box on the right.

Look up the word "big." What does the thesaurus say? Does it tell you to "see" another word? If so, what did you find when you looked up that other word? Maybe it didn't tell you to "see" another word. Try looking up one of the synonyms or antonyms for "big." What new words did you discover? Enter those words in the boxes you made in your notebook.

humongous

commodious

capacious

13

CHAPTER THREE

How to Use an Online Thesaurus

Now you know how to use a book thesaurus. Using an online thesaurus should be easy! The first thing you need to do is find a good Web site. Ask a trusted adult, such as a parent, teacher, or librarian, for help. Web sites that have a thesaurus may also have a dictionary. So make sure you're on the right part of the site! Sometimes the thesaurus is even a part of the dictionary. Get help if the Web site is confusing.

Sometimes using an online thesaurus is faster than using a printed thesaurus.

Most thesaurus Web sites have a blank box at the top of the screen. There you can type in the word you want to look up. Look to the left or right of the box. You might see the word "find," "look up," "go," or "search." Or there might be a picture of a magnifying glass next to the box. Type your word in the box. Hit the Enter button on the keyboard. Or click the mouse on those words beside the box. The thesaurus will quickly look up your word!

Pronounce as:
thi-SAWR-uhs

Hearing a word out
loud helps you learn
to say it the right
way.

From here, the online thesaurus is a
lot like the book thesaurus. It shows the
part of speech and the definition. It shows
synonyms, related words, near antonyms,
and antonyms. Sometimes it even tells you
how to **pronounce** a word. Then you will
know how to say it. Do you see a picture of a
speaker next to your word? Click on it with
your mouse. The computer will say the word
out loud to you!

Maybe you want to look up a word in the synonym or antonym list. It's easy when you're using an online thesaurus. A word that is underlined or colored blue is a link. That means you can click on it with your mouse. The link will take you to the part of the thesaurus that tells you about that word! Not all Web sites have words with links. So you might have to type in the word you like and look it up.

walk (verb) to move along by placing one foot on the ground before lifting the other

Synonyms: march, step, pace, stride

Related words: plod, stalk, patrol, parade

Near antonyms: trot, gallop, dart

Antonyms: run ←

Click on a word that is underlined. The computer will take you to the underlined word in the thesaurus.

Activity

Let's play a game of song synonyms using the nursery rhyme "Jack and Jill."

hill
fetch
pail
fell
broke
tumble
said

1. Write the words on the right on a page in your notebook. Put each word on a separate line, top to bottom.
2. Look up "hill" in an online thesaurus. Next to "hill" on your list, write a synonym you find.
3. Do the same for each word on the list. When you complete the list, put the synonyms into the spots where the original words were.
4. Then sing the song with the synonyms. It probably won't rhyme anymore. But you'll have lots of fun and learn a few new words, too!

Here's *Jack and Jill*, just in case you forgot it:

Jack and Jill went up the hill
To fetch a pail of water.
Jack fell down and broke his crown,
And Jill came tumbling after.

Then up got Jack
And said to Jill,
As in his arms he took her,
Let's fetch that pail of water.

bucket

So Jack and Jill went up the hill
To fetch the pail of water,
And took it home to Mother dear,
Who thanked her son and daughter.

To get a copy of this activity, visit www.cherrylakepublishing.com/activities.

CHAPTER FOUR

A New World of Words

Imagine how many new words you could learn by using a thesaurus! You want to tell someone that the dinosaur bones you

Look at those dinosaur bones! They are humongous!

Now you know how to find just the right words!

Using a thesaurus can help make the words you say and write more interesting.

saw were big. Now you would have all kinds of new ways to do that. You could say they were large, massive, or humongous! What if you saw small dinosaur bones? Then you could choose from the list of antonyms for the word "big." The words are waiting for you in the thesaurus!

Glossary

antonyms (AN-toh-nimz) words that mean the opposite of each other

definitions (de-fuh-NIH-shunz) explanations of the meaning of a word or phrase

near antonyms (NEER AN-toh-nimz) words that are almost the opposite of each other

pronounce (pruh-NOUNTS) to say words in a particular way

related words (ree-LAY-ted WORDS) words that mean almost, but not exactly, the same as each other

synonym (SIN-uh-nim) a word that means the same as another word

Be safe when exploring online!

Find Out More

BOOKS

Bollard, John. *Scholastic Pocket Thesaurus*. New York:
    Scholastic, Inc., 2005.

How to Use a Dictionary How to Use a Thesaurus. Springfield,
    MA: Federal Street Press, 2003.

WEB SITES

Merriam-Webster Word Central

www.wordcentral.com

You'll become a word wizard playing games with Alpha-bot, an animated robot who challenges you to fun spelling contests. His friend Robo-Bee will help your skills blossom as he takes you through his garden of synonyms, antonyms, and spelling puzzles!

Wordsmyth

www.wordsmyth.net

Check out this great online dictionary-thesaurus with special search tools for beginners and children. You'll find audio pronunciations, thousands of images and animations, and plenty of quizzes to test your word skills.

Index

About the Author

Kara Fribley is a graduate student at the University of Michigan specializing in School Library Media. She enjoys spending what spare time she gets with her husband, Dave.